Ruby Bridges

By Margaret Nevinski
Illustrated by Taylor Bruce

Ruby Bridges went up the steps of her new school.
Ruby was in first grade.

It was
November 14,
1960.

When Ruby was in first grade,
black and white children went
to different schools.
Only white children went to this school.

Many people wanted this to change.
They wanted black children
to go to this school, too.
Ruby was the first.

WILLIAM FRANTZ
PUBLIC SCHOOL

Ruby's school
in New Orleans

Other people did not want
black and white children
to go to school together.
When Ruby went to school,
they yelled at her.

Ruby held her mother's hand.
Her mother said,
"Don't be afraid."

Mrs. Henry

Ruby went inside.
She saw her teacher, Mrs. Henry.
She did not see any children.
Their families did not want them
in school with Ruby.

Every day, Ruby went to school.
Every day, the people yelled at her.

Every day, Mrs. Henry and
Ruby were all alone.

They read books.
They sang songs.

But every day,
Ruby ate lunch alone.

All year, people were trying
to change Ruby's school.
They wanted children
to go back to Ruby's class.

The next year, Ruby was
in second grade.
She did not see people yelling.
She saw other children.
Ruby was happy.
She had new friends.

Today, black and white children
go to school together.
Ruby Bridges helped to make
this change.